Become a SuperHero Manager:

The Common Sense 9 Step Guide

Douglas H. Johnson

ISBN: 978-1482611410

Table of Contents

Table of Contents (con't.)

Introduction

In the beginning...things were good...

God had just spent six days putting together a perfect world...his business...and then, wouldn't you know it - the first case of stupid people syndrome!

One simple directive (from someone whose directives obviously should be followed - the BOSS - God), and His employees Adam and Eve didn't follow it. So look where we are today! Was God a lousy manager, or was He, in fact, a SuperHero Manager? What do you think?

Part One

Stupid People Syndrome
In Business

An Epidemic of
Stupid People Syndrome

It is no wonder that one of the most popular words today is "Duh!"

That one word is a reflection of our times – a period during which there seems to be a rampant epidemic of stupid people syndrome.

Stupid people syndrome. That says it all – politely, perhaps, but nonetheless, it says it all: the driver who pulls out right in front of you when there is no one behind you, and then proceeds very slowly; the employee who asks you to schedule company training around an aerobics class during working hours – and no, this is not an employee benefit; or the server in a restaurant who does not give back change with which you can leave an appropriate tip.

What has happened to us? Many people say that our society is "dumbing down." Can this be true? How did it happen?

An explanation might be forthcoming in the following obituary, circulated on the internet. Unfortunately, the author is not known, or appropriate credit would be given.

Obituary of Common Sense

Today we mourn the passing of a beloved old friend by the name of Common Sense who has been with us for many years. No one knows for sure how old he was since his birth records were long ago lost in bureaucratic red tape.

He will be remembered as having cultivated such value lessons as knowing when to come in out of the rain, why the early bird gets the worm and that life isn't always fair.

Common Sense lived by simple, sound financial policies (don't spend more than you earn) and reliable parenting strategies (adults, not kids, are in charge).

His health began to rapidly deteriorate when well intentioned but overbearing regulations were set in place.

Reports of a six-year-old boy charged with sexual harassment for kissing a classmate; teens suspended from school for using mouthwash after lunch; and a teacher fired for reprimanding an unruly student, only worsened his condition.

It declined even further when schools were required to get parental consent to administer aspirin to a student; but, could not inform the parents when a student became pregnant and wanted to have an abortion.

Finally, Common Sense lost the will to live as the Ten Commandments became contraband; churches became businesses; and criminals received better treatment than their victims.

Common Sense finally gave up the ghost after a woman failed to realize that a steaming cup of coffee was hot, she spilled a bit in her lap, and was awarded a huge settlement.

Common Sense was preceded in death by his parents, Truth and Trust; his wife, Discretion; his daughter, Responsibility; and his son, Reason.

He is survived by two stepbrothers: My Rights and Ima Whiner.

Not many attended his funeral because so few realized he was gone. If you still know him pass this on; if not, join the majority and do nothing.

Now, what does all of this have to do with managing a business? Well, everything!

Why People Today Exhibit "Stupid People Syndrome"

Common sense is societal. This means that as society changes, the ability and/or desire to have common sense also changes. Common sense has always been a trait of independent, self-reliant people. The "New Deal" of the 1930's tended to discourage self-reliance. Therefore, as people became more dependent on government, they became less dependent on themselves, thereby lessening the need to possess common sense. As the need for common sense decreased, people started to exhibit symptoms of stupid people syndrome. The best (and most polite) way we know of to define stupid people syndrome can be expressed in one word – "Duh!"

Today, some people feel like they already know what they need to know, so they are closed to having new experiences. Because experience, as we will discover later, is one of the keys to having common sense, the lack of common sense becomes as much of an attitude issue as it is an ability issue.

> *"Everybody gets so much information all day long*
> *that they lose their common sense."*
> *Gertrude Stein*

Another reason people today don't seem to have common sense is the "theory of memes." Introduced in Richard Dawkins' book *The Selfish Gene* and discussed by Leon Felkins in 1996, memes are explanations or excuses used to explain away the complexities of the world, and therefore the need for common sense. An example of a meme would explain that persons in dire financial straits no longer need to worry because the government can somehow magically create money to pay for any social inconvenience. As memes become more prevalent, the need to use common sense becomes less necessary.

In today's world, the "politically correct" meme cluster often is in direct conflict with common sense. For instance, common sense would tell some males that if the female working next to him were incredibly sexy, he should do something about it.

Political correctness, on the other hand, would put a stop to that behavior before it happens. So, if the male figures out that common sense could get him into trouble, how often is he going to use it? Please note here, that if he thought through all of the implications of his common sense actions, as we will learn in the next section, he would reach the same conclusions as if following the "politically correct" meme cluster.

As a society, we have become too reliant on someone else warning us of consequences rather than thinking of them on our own. Warning labels present some of the best examples of stupid people syndrome at work. Do we really have to be warned about things that should be common sense? Obviously so! There is even a contest called the Wacky Warning Label Contest. Conducted annually by the Michigan Lawsuit Abuse Watch, M-LAW, the contest entries reveal how a lack of common sense on the part of consumers has forced manufacturers to put warning labels on products to reduce liability. For example, actual warning labels have said:

- on a hairdryer: "Don't drop your hairdryer in a bathtub full of water – electricity and water don't mix!"
- on a household iron: "Never iron clothes while they are being worn."
- on a bottle of drain cleaner: "If you do not understand, or cannot read, all directions, cautions and warnings, do not use this product."

And so it goes!

Could Stupid People Syndrome Be Killing Profits in Your Business?

The effects of stupid people syndrome are many and varied. In business, however, just one instance of stupid people syndrome can cause the loss of a valuable customer, cost extra money in the manufacturing process, or delay shipment of a product. Any or all of these can lead to frustration, rage, disappointment, and, obviously, loss of business or profit.

There are seven basic benefits of common sense for business. All other benefits, if you think about it, fall under one of these seven areas:

- *Common sense improves productivity.* As business owners/managers, do we not want the productivity of ourselves and our employees at the highest levels they can be? Of course we do!

- *Common sense improves problem solving and decision making skills.* If these skills were in place, would our lives not be much easier? Imagine, new products or services, improved time lines, and a smoother running operation could be ours if our employees were empowered to solve problems and make decisions on their own.

- *Common sense improves customer service and customer satisfaction.* Hum, what business owner/manager would not want this?

- *Common sense improves common courtesy.* In today's society, common courtesy is all too rare. We are all too much in a hurry, too self-absorbed, too non-caring to practice courtesy. What a refreshing change – and your customers will remember!

- *Common sense improves morale and increases self-esteem.* Those of us who have been in management roles understand how important these traits are for having a productive workforce. Gone are the days of the manager's "my way or the highway." A happy workforce with good self-esteem can take your business to the top!

- *Common sense improves truth, values and simplicity of life.* Today, we are involved in the "back to the earth" movement, the "green" movement, and the "simple is better" movement. Doesn't it make sense that truth, values and simplicity of life in your business can help it perform better?

- *Common sense improves seeing things as they are and doing things as they should be done.* Enough said!

Does Your Business Show Signs of Stupid People Syndrome?

There are many ways to know if your business is feeling the effects of stupid people syndrome.

For example:

- Have you noticed business dropping off?
- Have you seen your customers treated rudely by your employees?
- Have you noticed a lack of phone calls?
- Have you maintained the same way of doing things for a number of years?

Have you done a self-evaluation of your business?

A self-evaluation is probably the simplest and least expensive technique for discovering if your business shows signs of stupid people syndrome.

A self-evaluation puts you in the place of your external customer, or internal customer, the employee. How is your business perceived, because we all know that perception is reality?

The following are some questions that you may want to ask yourself in a self-evaluation. Mind you, these are only some questions. Ask yourself others that are appropriate to your business.

- Have you ever tried to call your own business on the telephone line a customer would use? If you do that, do you get caught in "voice mail hell?"
- As you approach the parking lot, is it neat and clean? Translation – would you want to do business with a slob?
- How do you manage your employees – are you dictatorial or interactive? Note - you may want to get a second opinion on this one.
- Do you have a business plan that you have shared with your employees so that they know the company's mission and how to best follow it?
- Do you make "zero-based decisions?" What, you don't know what a "zero-based decision" is? We'll cover that later.

Real Life Examples of Stupid People Syndrome in Business

The following stories are all true. As you read each one, see how it (or something like it) could apply to your business. Think about the HUGE impact that even small issues like these can have on your organization. Have you become enough of a SuperHero Manager yet to have recognized and done something about these issues already?

Case of the Vanity License Plates

A local merchant, very proud of his business, has affixed magnetic signs advertising his company's name to the sides of his vehicle. This truck is parked in front of the door of this retail establishment all day.

As one comes around the front of the truck in order to enter the business, the vanity license plate becomes visible. It reads simply "go awy."

Lesson to be learned: "go awy" (go away) is not particularly the sentiment one wants to express while trying to entice customers and potential customers into the facility! The brain is in conflict here, because the magnetic signs on the side of the truck are an invitation to enter the business. The license plates, on the other hand, are a not-so-subtle invitation to leave. (Think: A SuperHero Manager thinks of the darndest things and STOPS and THINKS before acting.)

Case of the Lost Tip

A customer at a restaurant is given a $10 tab. As he pulls out his wallet to pay, he makes the comment to the server that the only bill he has in his wallet is a twenty. The server leaves to make change, and returns with a ten dollar bill.

The customer, annoyed by the fact that the server did not bring back "appropriate" change, says to the server, "Your tip this time will be a 'tip'. Let's discuss what just happened here...I normally leave, and you normally expect, a tip of 15-20% of the tab. That would be $1.50 to $2.00, correct?" After the server agrees with his math, the customer continues. "Now, if you give me a ten dollar bill as change, I have three options: 1. To ask you to give me change for the ten dollar bill, 2. To leave you a tip of $10, (a 100% tip), or 3. To leave you no tip. Which option does your common sense tell you I probably will do?"

Lesson to be learned: At this point, the server realizes that the best way to ensure a proper tip is to return appropriate change, in this case a five and five singles. This is how common sense works. It also points out the fact that this server could have been trained much better, increasing his(her) morale and self-esteem. (Think: A SuperHero Manager trains his(her) employees well.)

Case of Voice Mail Hell

Every time I called a particular client, the phone was answered by an "automatic attendant." Before I knew it, I would be caught in "voice mail hell," you know, that place where you must listen to the menu of choices, pick "1", "2" or "3", then find that you are in a loop from which you cannot escape.

One more time, the owner of this company was telling me how customer friendly his company was and how he prided himself on always being accessible to the customer. Rather than argue, I dialed the company's phone number on my cellphone and handed it to him with the simple directive to try to get through to himself. About two minutes later.......

Lesson to be learned: Put yourself in your customer's place. How many customers, or potential customers, have been lost because they don't have the patience to put up with "voice mail hell?" (Think: A SuperHero Manager tests his(her) systems.)

Case of the Chewed Pen

My wife and I went out to eat at a very classy restaurant, known for its great food and service.

We enjoyed our evening. The food was absolutely wonderful, the service impeccable, and then we got our check - you know, the check presented in a little black book - the one delivered with a pen so that you may sign the credit card slip.

Let's talk about the pen here – probably a 29 cent pen – about three inches in length – with teeth marks all around the top! Someone had obviously been chewing on this pen in between customers. Needless to say, this was at the opposite end of the spectrum from the rest of our experience.

Upon leaving, I said something to the manager about what a great evening we had had – except for the poor "taste in our mouth" that the chewed off pen had left with us. I suggested perhaps a new pen and a word to the servers would be appropriate – and – he blew me off!

Lesson to be learned: Listen to your customers. Sometimes, just sometimes, they may give you some valuable information to help keep you from losing other customers.

Needless to say, we haven't been back to that restaurant. And, do you know how many times I have told this story? Unfortunately for the restaurant, a number of folks have figured out its name – and won't go there either! (Think: A SuperHero Manager listens to his(her) customers.)

Case of the "Blowtorch, Knife or Scissors"

Watching a segment on the morning news show "Good Morning America," I heard the great news that several large companies, including Sony and Amazon, were likely to come out soon with new packaging that doesn't require a blowtorch, knife or scissors to open.

Quoted was Jeff Bezos of Amazon who said that he decided to investigate packaging after having difficulty opening some items. According to the American Safety Commission, some 6,000 Americans visit an emergency room every year after trying to open a package.

Lesson to be learned: Well, duh, why has this taken so long? Most consumers have been complaining about this problem for years! (Think: A SuperHero Manager listens to his(her) customers!)

Case of the Clean Tables

Don't you hate it when you're eating in a restaurant and a person comes over to a table near you and sprays it with a strong smelling cleanser?

Okay, okay, I know the tables should be cleaned. And I have no problem with that. But I also know that there are cleaners out there that are antimicrobial disinfectants and deodorizers produced specifically for use in restaurants and hospitals that have NO odor! And I know this because I am holding a container of it in my hand!

Talking about that spray, the entry to a restaurant we visited once leads customers straight into a bookcase. This is confusing, because it is the first thing seen upon entering the restaurant. AND, on the shelves of the bookcase are prominently displayed...you guessed it – a bottle of that spray and a dirty cloth used to wipe down the tables.

Lesson to be learned: Perception is reality! Think about it – do you really want to eat in a restaurant where you are greeted by a bottle of cleaner and a dirty rag? Again, how many customers, or potential customers, have been lost because of this? (Think: A SuperHero Manager knows that perception is reality, and that this reality may not be good!)

Case of the Long Name

When naming your business, make the name short enough to fit easily on business cards or business nametags, often used when attending an event.

For example, *DHJ Business Writers and Website Developers with an Attitude Inc.,* just doesn't fit on one of those "Hello, I'm..." sticky nametags. So, if all that fits is "DHJ Business," do the other attendees really know who or what your business is?

And, for goodness sakes, don't start the business name with the word "THE." Where does that name get filed – under "The" or under the first real word? Check it out – everyone has a different method. So if you want your company to be found in a list, name it so the name makes sense.

I also heard a complaint recently from a business owner who said that no one knew that his business was a CPA firm. The name? Three last names strung together with nothing more than an Inc. after them - Johnson, St. Germain and Bibby Inc. - name made up to protect the guilty.

Lesson to be learned: When naming your business, think of the implications of the name. Will people know what your business does, is it easy to remember, and does it fit easily on a card or on an application?

Is your crystal ball turned on? (Think: A SuperHero Manager thinks through the implications before making a decision.)

Case of the Ignoring Hosts

I don't think I have the highest of standards when eating out. However, when I walk into a restaurant that requires at least three host(ess)es who totally ignore customers as they walk in, yet continue to converse among themselves, I do have a bit of a problem.

Lesson to be learned: Have they read their job description? Do they know what customer service is? Were they trained at all by someone who "gives a damn" about the customer? Do they know the consequences when a customer who has been ignored spreads that word to all of his(her) friends?

I think not! (Think: A SuperHero Manager staffs appropriately and trains well.)

Case of the "SWAG" Method of Pricing

A client and I were discussing one of his company's products. I thought the price was very low and made a comment to him about it. He responded with "Well, I lose a little bit on each item, but I make it up in volume." Seriously.

Upon further discussion (about two hours' worth), we discovered that he had no idea of his overhead or cost of goods and was pricing the product using the "SWAG" method – the "Scientific Wild Ass Guess" method.

Lesson to be learned: When pricing your goods or services, know your costs and build in your profit. As we all know (okay, maybe not this client), if you lose a little bit on each item, you will lose a whole lot in volume! (Think: A SuperHero Manager knows his(her) costs and prices accordingly.)

Case of the Whipped Cream in Hot Chocolate

A friend of mine decided to splurge and order a hot chocolate with SKIM milk at a local coffee shop. When the lid was opened, lo and behold! There was a huge blob of whipped cream sitting on top of that hot chocolate! Talk about a splurge!

Lesson to be learned: There normally is a reason one orders what they do – it is the job of the barista, in this case, to produce what was ordered. Was there a particular reason skim milk was ordered rather than whipped cream? Or was the barista just not paying attention to the customer? Whatever the reason, the customer did not get what he wanted – not a good thing in a retail business! (Think: A SuperHero Manager trains his(her) employees to listen to the customer!)

Case of a Full-Service Gas Station – We Wash Customers, Too!

I was at a gas station, filling up my car's tank, when I noticed a young female employee come out the front sliding door of the station with a bucket of water that obviously had been used to clean the floor inside.

It was quite cold out. She took about two steps from the doorway, and then threw the bucket of water straight ahead onto the entryway without seeming to pay attention to what she was doing. She narrowly missed a patron who had just gotten out of her car and was on her way into the store.

Two things occurred to me: that the water was going to freeze on contact with the cement entryway to the station because it was so cold, causing a hazard to customers; and that the water was filthy - not a very welcoming sight to the facility, nor to the woman almost hit by the "flying water."

Lesson to be learned: Think, think, think and even though it seems like common sense, train, train, train – never throw your cleaning water out the front door of your business! (Think: A SuperHero Manager trains his(her) employees well.)

Case of the Status Automobiles

You know how some high class auto dealerships provide courtesy rides and loaner automobiles when your car is "in the shop?"

Well, not long ago I saw a local Mercedes-Benz dealership advertising its "Courtesy Auto Service" - on a more than slightly used, American-made minivan, showing lots of rust. Um, ok, I'm impressed - high-end automobile, right?

Then I got to thinking. I had also seen a GMC vehicle that was being used to advertise a BMW mechanic - and BMW's are the only make of car this particular mechanic works on. What's wrong with this picture?

Lesson to be learned: Think about the perception of everything you do. Luxury products should be represented by the perception of luxury, correct? (Think: A SuperHero Manager is aware of the power of perception - it really can make a difference!)

Case of the Inappropriate E-mail Address

Somehow, using an e-mail address such as
<u>PartyAnimal@PartyLikeThereIsNoTomorrow.com</u> as your business
e-mail address just does not seem appropriate unless, of course, you are
selling party favors.

Lesson to be learned: Think about it – your email address can (and
does) say a whole lot about you. (Think: A SuperHero Manager
realizes the implications of even the smallest details.)

Case of the Lip-Shaped Urinals

In 2004, Virgin Airways decided to install bright red women's mouth shaped urinals in the men's restrooms at John F. Kennedy International Airport in New York. When plans were made public, a spokesperson for Virgin Airways said that the airlines were surprised at the outcry from outraged patrons. They decided to scrap the plan.

Lesson to be learned: Really? (Think: A SuperHero Manager thinks of perceptions, implications, reactions...do I need to continue? Dumb idea!!)

And while we're talking about men's rooms:

Case of Doing Business in a Stall or Multi-Tasking at its Finest

In a men's room; on a cell phone; loud (maybe that was to cover up the flushing and other liquid and non-liquid sounds!)

Anyway, picture this – ah, no, don't picture this!

At a rest stop along the highway, and during a visit to the men's room, I was fortunate(?) enough to be privy to a one-sided conversation about how sales were down, the boss was a bastard, and how if he (the man in the stall) ran the company, he would change the sales model. And that's the short version!

Not to mention the germs on that phone...

Really, you call that multi-tasking?

Lesson to be learned: Who knows who may be listening in on a conversation: a customer, a potential customer, or the boss. Need I say more? One last word – perception – would you do business with that company? (Think: A SuperHero Manager can't control everything – but "hire right, manage right" can sure help!)

So, let's summarize some lessons from the preceding stories that a SuperHero Manager may use to prevent symptoms of stupid people syndrome in his(her) business:

A SuperHero Manager thinks of the darndest things – (s)he STOPS and THINKS before acting!

A SuperHero Manager trains his(her) employees well.

A SuperHero Manager tests his(her) systems.

A SuperHero Manager listens to his(her) customers.

A SuperHero Manager listens to his(her) customers - think this might be important?

A SuperHero Manager knows that perception is reality, and that this reality may not be good!

A SuperHero Manager thinks through the implications before making a decision.

A SuperHero Manager staffs appropriately and trains well.

A SuperHero Manager knows his(her) costs and prices accordingly.

A SuperHero Manager trains his(her) employees to listen to the customer!

A SuperHero Manager trains his(her) employees well – this is important, too!

A SuperHero Manager is aware of the power of perception – it really can make a difference!

A SuperHero Manager realizes the implications of even the smallest details.

A SuperHero Manager thinks of perceptions, implications and reactions.

A SuperHero Manager can't control everything – but "hire right, manage right" can sure help!

I Don't Have Stupid People Syndrome – It Must Be My Employees

Thought so!

We hear this so often, and upon investigation, normally find that the company is facing some challenges that could be resolved with some common sense "attitude adjustment." And what is that exactly?

Think about it. If you have made the statement (or even thought) "I don't have stupid people syndrome – it must be my employees," and you own or manage the company, you are probably the one in need of an attitude adjustment.

You set the stage for the performance. If you think your employees are showing symptoms of stupid people syndrome, you don't need to look very far to discover the reason why. Employees follow the example set by their supervisor, boss, owner or manager. (Translation: YOU are the reason your employees are showing symptoms of stupid people syndrome!)

Part Two

The Common Sense Cure

Okay, What Is Common Sense, Anyway?

"Common sense" is a hard term to define. Many people, when asked, will say that although not clearly able to define common sense, they know it when they see it. A SuperHero Manager definitely knows it when (s)he sees it, *and* also practices it in daily business life.

To help us define *common sense,* let's begin with *Webster's Dictionary:*

1. Originally, the faculty which supposedly united and interpreted impressions of the five senses, hence
2. Practical judgment or intelligence; ordinary good sense.

The American Heritage® Dictionary of the English Language defines *common sense* simply as native good judgment. [Translation of Latin *sênsus commúnis,* common feelings of humanity.]

Wiktionary defines *common sense* as:

1. (obsolete) An internal sense, formerly believed to be the sense by which information from the other five senses is understood and interpreted. ⬜
2. Ordinary sensible understanding; one's basic intelligence which allows for plain understanding and without which good decisions or judgments cannot be made.

Others have said of common sense:

- Common sense is sound practical judgment that is independent of specialized knowledge, training, or the like; normal native intelligence.

- Common sense is the combination of truth, values, and simplicity.

- Common sense is the art of resolving questions.

- Common sense is the ability to apply information in productive and meaningful ways.

- Common sense is often referred to as having good judgment, or horsesense.

- Practical common sense sees things as they are and does things as they should be done.

"Common Sense is genius
dressed in its working clothes."
Ralph Waldo Emerson

About Common Sense

Common sense is that genius of mankind, which when properly directed, is the one attribute that will carry mankind through the perplexities of life. (from *The Well Tempered Hunch*, Conrad Hilton)

Common sense varies in character, according to surroundings and education.

Common sense is domain specific: in other words, a person might use a lot of common sense on the job, but not at home, or vice-versa.

People with common sense tend to be individualists and tend to be self-reliant.

There is a "spectrum of usage" pertaining to common sense. Common sense, on one end of the spectrum, is often displayed by people who live simple (many times rural) lives. These people tend to be those who are very independent and often self-reliant. At the other end of the spectrum are people involved with technology. These people also generally display very logical, commonsensical tendencies. In the middle of the spectrum are those who may often display the characteristics of stupid people syndrome. They use very little common sense in certain circumstances (domains). For example, they may pull out right in front of your car from a side road or driveway when there are no other cars in sight.

Common sense is at times exhibited in some forms of humor. Maine residents, often called 'downeasters', are often noted for their use of common sense humor, even though they do not mean to be funny. They appear to be funny, however, because of their directness, their honesty, and a short, concise speech form mixed with an extraordinary amount of perceptiveness.

Following are examples of downeast humor from *A Collection of Maine Humor* by Bill Sawyer:

> Tourist to Maine resident: "Think it's going to stop raining?"
> Maine resident: "Always has!"

> Asked a fellow in Jonesport if he's lived there all his life.
> "Not yet," he said.

> While picking up his mail, a visitor from New Jersey said to the postmaster, "You sure got a lot of old folk up here. What's your mortality rate?"
> "Just like it's always been...one per person."

Of Course I Can Score Well on a Common Sense Test

I run the company.

Really! Okay, see how you do on this easy test!

Easy Test for Generic Common Sense

Please choose the best answer for each question.

1. Your business is to place a sign, approximately 4 feet by 8 feet in size, next to a driveway. Where would you place it?

    A. location A

    B. location B

    C. location C

2. If you are a customer in a restaurant, and your check is for $10, you reach into your wallet and all you have is a $20 bill. You mention this as you give the bill to the server. What should the server give you as change?

    A. a $10 bill

    B. ten singles

    C. a five and five singles

3. You are in your car waiting to turn a corner. There is a car coming toward you at a fairly high speed, but there are no cars behind that one. You

    A. pull out in front of the car

    B. pull out after the car passes by

    C. sit until you see another car coming and pull out in front of it.

4. You are sitting in your office and the phone rings. You

    A. let it ring

    B. answer it

    C. wait for someone else to answer it

5. You have just been complimented on the sweater you are wearing. You

    A. never wear it again

    B. wear it again soon

    C. give it to someone else to wear

6. You know that ice should be at least four inches thick before you venture out onto it. You have just come across a pond that looks like a great place to skate. You

    A. put on your skates and skate out to the middle of the pond
    B. try to determine the thickness of the ice
    C. stand on the ice to see if it holds you

7. You are cooking dinner, but you have forgotten if you turned on the right-hand, back burner. In order to find out, you

    A. put your hand on each burner to see if any are hot
    B. assume that none are on, and turn them all on
    C. look at the light indicator that is on the stove showing which burners are on

8. You are in a hurry, and the line in the Post Office is rather long. You must mail a letter today, so you

    A. mail the letter without a stamp
    B. wait in line, making you late for an appointment
    C. decide to come back later

9. You decide to clean the leaves out of your gutters. You

    A. find a ladder that is the appropriate size, position it against your house, and clean the gutter

    B. climb onto the roof, and walk along the edge, trying to remove leaves as you go

    C. decide that the gutters really don't need cleaning, although you can see leaves in them, and do something else

10. You decide to donate some books to your local library. You have approximately 20 hardback books, and you

    A. put them in a paper bag to carry

    B. put them in a box to carry

    C. pick them up in your arms in one load and carry them

You're kidding, right? You really need the answers? Okay, okay, look at the next page - and don't even ask why the answers are on the next page!

Answer Key:

1. A: location A allows the best visibility

2. C: a five and five singles

3. B: pull out after the car passes by

4. B: answer it

5. B: wear it again soon

6. B: try to determine the thickness of the ice

7. C: look at the light indicator that is on the stove showing which burners are on

8. C: decide to come back later

9. A: find a ladder that is the appropriate size, position it against your house, and clean the gutter

10. B: put them in a box to carry

Why Is Common Sense Important in Business?

There are several traits that make common sense important to business:

- Common sense helps provide a means of living that is simple, direct, and easy to understand. Remember KISS? That's Keep It Simple, Stupid – and it makes living (and working) a whole lot easier!

- Common sense leads to common courtesy.

- Common sense helps provide harmony in life, which makes people happy. Remember, a "happy employee is a productive employee!"

What are the benefits of using common sense in business?

- customers expect common sense
- customers deserve common sense
- customers have often done without common sense too long
- customers will continue to demand common sense
- customers will take their business elsewhere if they don't get common sense

Using Common Sense to Run Your Business – A Simple Self-Evaluation

Use this simple self-evaluation to start you on the road to using "the common sense cure" in your business. As you answer each question, think about why it is being asked and the implications of your answers. (Think like a SuperHero Manager.) Most questions are based on things that should be happening in your business.

Self-Evaluation for Business Common Sense

	Yes	No
1. Does your company have a mission statement?	☐	☐

2. If yes, please write it here.

| 3. Does your company make *every* decision based on whether it meets the mission statement? | ☐ | ☐ |

4. What size is your company?

	Yes	No
small	☐	☐
medium	☐	☐
large	☐	☐

	Yes	No

5. What is the culture of your company?

(check each that applies)

	Yes	No
formal	☐	☐
informal	☐	☐
corporate	☐	☐
casual	☐	☐

6. Do you consider your company to be (check each that applies):

	Yes	No
employee friendly	☐	☐
customer friendly	☐	☐
vendor friendly	☐	☐

7. Is background music played at your company?   ☐   ☐

	Yes	No
8. If so, what type?		
classical	☐	☐
rock (any type)	☐	☐
country	☐	☐
easy listening	☐	☐
9. Does your company have internal customers?	☐	☐
10. Would you say that your employees generally speak:		
at each other	☐	☐
to each other	☐	☐
with each other	☐	☐
11. Are employees encouraged?	☐	☐
12. Are employees empowered?	☐	☐

	Yes	No
13. Is each employee a quality control specialist?	☐	☐
14. Are your employees rewarded with something other than cash when they do a good job?	☐	☐

15. Who makes decisions about day-to-day
situations (check each that applies)?

	Yes	No
employees	☐	☐
managers	☐	☐
owners	☐	☐

	Yes	No
16. Does your company practice continuous improvement?	☐	☐
17. Does your company practice creativity?	☐	☐
18. Is every employee policy and procedure consistent with the corporate culture of your company?	☐	☐

	Yes	No

19. Is every operational policy and procedure
consistent with the corporate culture of your
company? ☐ ☐

20. Does every policy and procedure help you
meet your company's mission statement? ☐ ☐

Scoring

Score one point for every "Yes" answer for questions #1 through #20.

Score one point for each box checked in question #6.

Score one point if the box "with one another" is checked in question #10.

Score one point for each box checked in question #15.

Add your scores.

Interpretation of Score:

If your company received a score of 15 to 20, chances are your company uses common sense on a regular basis. This is a good thing and you are well on your way to becoming a SuperHero Manager!

If your company received a score of 7 to 14, chances are your company should use common sense on a more regular basis. More work is needed on your way to becoming a SuperHero Manager!

If your company received a score of 0 to 6, chances are your company could benefit from formal training in the use of common sense. It's still within your grasp! Much work is needed on your way to becoming a SuperHero Manager!

So, does your company practice common sense?

Disclaimer

This self-evaluation is meant to identify the level of use of common sense in your corporate setting. Answers will vary according to one's position with the company.

Only those persons licensed by Common Sense University should officially interpret your score. Failure to heed this warning may lead to examples of stupid people syndrome.

Common Sense During the Daily Grind – The Easy 9 Step Guide

You know, something often sounds great – until you try to put it into practice, that is. So, the next portion of this book is devoted to living what we're preaching here – how to use common sense in all matters to cure the stupid people syndrome in your business on your journey to becoming a SuperHero Manager.

You Can't Get There
If You Don't Know Where You're Going

Introduction

Now, think about it. You are about to take a trip. Do you know your final destination? Yes, of course you do. And since you know what that destination is, you can plan your route to get you there. Conversely, if you don't know where you are going, how do you plan your route? It's pretty difficult.

The same holds true for just about anything in the business world. If you don't know where you're going, if you don't know what your goals are, if you don't know what your niche market is, if you don't know how to make your widget, how will you guide your business? If you do know that in three years, you want your business to sell $1,000,000 worth of faux leather car seat covers to owners of pre-1960 British sport car owners, then you can develop your plan to achieve that goal. You have to know where you're going in order to figure out how to get there!

Deciding on a Destination

The first thing you must do is to decide on a destination. What are your goals?

The following are some points to know about setting goals, and these will help you on your journey.

- goals should be measurable
- goals should be attainable
  - goals produce either reinforcement or punishment (either you achieve them or you don't)
- goals should be set that increase opportunities to receive positive reinforcement. Therefore, there should be many goals, not few.
- the fastest way to improve a behavior (move toward your goal) is to positively reinforce small successive successful changes towards that goal (called shaping behavior)

Planning the Trip

In order to attain your goals (reach your destination), you must do some planning:

- know the expectations

    o   there may be detours (or setbacks) along the way

    o   there may be rough roads

    o   it may take longer than you think to get there

    o   you **will** get there

- making reservations - planning your days

    o   know your route

    o   know your stops on the way

    o   know when you have arrived

Stops Along the Way

- **dealing with people.** You mean I have to deal with co-workers on the way? You bet, and following are the skills and abilities you need:
  - communication
    - be open
    - be honest
    - be discreet (if need be)
    - be considerate of the other person's feelings
    - be positive (even in a negative situation)
      - reprimand from the *One Minute Manager* by Blanchard and Johnson
        - 30 seconds of discussing the problem specifically
        - 5 seconds of silence
        - 25 seconds of positive reinforcement and encouragement
  - fairness
  - consistency
    - be aware of the implications of what you say, imply or do to all

○   trust - what more can I say? People innately want to do the right thing - just give them a chance until they prove otherwise.

○   self-esteem (I know, I'm tired of this word, too, so let's call it confidence in oneself)

- ways to build confidence in oneself:
  - ○ visualize success
  - ○ be nice to yourself - you're not as bad as you think!
  - ○ find little things that you do well (or things that others think you do well) - focus on the positive
  - ○ be true to yourself - do what you think is right
  - ○ try to improve one thing about yourself every day
  - ○ exercise - not only your body, but your brain! You'll be surprised how good it feels.
  - ○ relax - you don't need to be perfect. (Do you really know anyone who is?) Just try your best!

- o look at problems (or mistakes) objectively, not as a reflection of you, the person. Just because you have a problem, or have made a mistake, does not make you a bad person, it just means that there is a problem to solve, or a mistake to correct.
- o flexibility - according to Webster, the ability to adapt to change - not a bad way to be if you're trying to get along with people
- o sense of humor - probably one of the easiest ways to get along with people
  - be able to laugh with others
  - be able to laugh at a situation
  - be able to laugh at yourself
  - lighten up! No one likes a grouch - and besides, what's the point? Life is too short not to enjoy it.
- o use of positive reinforcement
  - remember the expression that you get more flies with honey than you do with vinegar? It's true.
  - positive reinforcement is easy to do. Just watch someone doing something right.

Then tell them how much you like it, what a good job they're doing, how much you appreciate it, etc. etc. etc.

- **solving problems.** Do I really have to think, too? Simple ways to solve problems include:
  - o making zero based decisions
    - know the real problem we are trying to solve
    - know the facts
    - know what can be done to solve the problem, resolve the issue, or deal with it: in other words, brainstorm.
    - use common sense to make some zero based decisions. Zero based decisions are those that are the best decisions possible if there were no pre-existing conditions. When the best decision is determined, start factoring in the pre-existing conditions. Think of the effects of the decision - of actions, thoughts, words and deeds - on those who could possibly be affected by the decision.

- **using lateral thinking**
    - a different way of looking at the same thing (for example, thinking not affected by pre-conceived ideas or biases - a policeman did not arrest a man going the wrong way down a one way street. Why?

- **using continuous improvement**
    - the process of always trying to improve what it is that you are doing by thinking, re-studying, and being flexible enough to make changes

Games to Play Enroute

The following are some exercises for your brain. Are you serious? I thought this was supposed to teach me to have fun on the job! Yes, it is. And the more in shape your brain is, the more fun you will have on the job, and the better you will be at it!

Solve the equations:

A. 12 = S. of the Z.

B. 54 = C. in a D. (With the J.)

C. 57 = H. V.

D. 200 = D. for P. G. in M.

What is the hidden meaning of each set of words?

A.   B.

| belt

hitting |

| night   fly |

Lateral thinking exercises:

A man was drinking a cup of tea when he was suddenly blinded. How?

A blind beggar had a brother who died. What relation was the blind beggar to the brother who died? (The beggar was not his brother. How could this be?)

Understanding other points of view:

Picture each point of view:

There is an error on a bank customer's statement. Act out in your mind the reaction of the customer, the bank person the customer told of the error, the person who made the error, and that person's supervisor.

Brainteasers:

A. You wake up one morning and there is a power outage. You know you have 12 black socks and 10 brown ones in your drawer. What is the maximum number of socks you need to pull out before you are sure you have a match?

B. You are trying to get to Truthtown. You come to a fork in the road. One road leads to Truthtown (where everyone tells the truth), the other leads to Liartown (where everyone lies). At the fork is a man from one of those towns - but you don't know which one. You may ask him one question to find your way. What is that question?

Answer key

Solve the equations:

A. 12 = Signs of the Zodiac

B. 54 = Cards in a Deck with Jokers

C. 57 = Heinz Varieties

D. 200 = Dollars for Passing Go in Monopoly

Hidden Meanings:

A. hitting below the belt

B. fly by night

Lateral thinking exercises:

A. He had left his teaspoon in the cup of tea, and when he raised the cup to drink, the handle struck him in the eye and he was temporarily blinded.

B. The blind beggar was the sister of her brother who died.

Brainteasers:

A. 3

B. Ask the man which way is your hometown? Then go whichever way he points: if he's from Liartown, he'll point to Truthtown and if he's from Truthtown, well, you get it.

Arrival

You know you have reached your destination when your feelings change from

TGIF

(Thank Goodness It's Friday)

to

TGIM

(Thank Goodness It's Monday)

Arrival at the destination. Are we having fun yet?

References

Please note: Much research information for this section was gleaned from the following books and articles. They are also suggested reading for additional information.

Kane, Kate, *The Riddle of Job Interviews*, *Fast Company*, Premiere issue

Sloane & MacHale, *Great Lateral Thinking Puzzles*, Sterling Publishing Co., Inc. New York

Albrecht, Karl, *Brain Power - Learn to Improve Your Thinking Skills*, Simon & Schuster, New York

Newstrom & Scannell, *The Big Book of Business Games*, McGraw-Hill, New York

Daniels, Aubrey, *Bringing Out the Best in People*, McGraw-Hill, New York

Good Employees Are Hard to Find

Hire Right, Manage Right. This is probably THE most important common sense cure for stupid people syndrome in your organization. We hear all the time (and it's true from personal experience) that the people who work for you ARE your business. Everything flows from them – your products/services, your customers, your sales, your profits. In addition to hiring the right people, you must also manage them right!

How to Hire Right:
Interview Guidelines for the Regular Guy (Girl)

Okay, here's the situation. You have been asked to interview a candidate for a position with the company you work for, and you don't have a clue how to start. The following are some common sense pointers that will keep you on the right track. And remember, the more interviews you conduct, the more comfortable you will be doing them.

PURPOSE: The purpose of an interview is to receive information, give information, and promote good will.

OBJECTIVE: To select the most suitable individual for the available position.

The How-To's:

A. Prepare for the interview

1. Know the job for which you are interviewing, the daily duties and responsibilities and the extras you may want or need from time to time.

2. Review the resumes/applications. Look for items on the resumes/applications that are a match for the job.
   Hint: Just because someone doesn't have direct matches doesn't mean that there are none. Many skills exhibited in a previous job will transfer to the job for which you are hiring.

3. Think of your interview questions. Know these in advance - you should ask all candidates basically the same questions, so you can compare their qualifications "apples to apples." Remember, though, that you should also ask follow-up questions triggered by a candidate's response or that may only apply to that candidate.

4.   Choose your setting. Pick a place that will
     have a minimum of distractions, whether it is
     an office, or a corner of a table in the
     lunchroom at a fairly quiet time of day. You
     do not have to sit across from the person (as in
     opposite sides of a desk); in fact, it is often
     preferable to sit in a chair next to the person. This
     puts them more at ease, and creates a
     supportive atmosphere that will encourage
     them to be open and to give you the
     information you need to make a good
     decision.

B. Easy Tips for a Successful Interview

1.   Be on time for the interview yourself, introduce yourself
     as you shake the candidate's hand, greet the candidate
     briefly (ex. "Did you have any problem finding the
     plant?"), and sit down. Make sure the candidate is at
     ease. (See above.)
     Hint: Remember, while you are trying to determine if
     you want to hire this person, they should be trying to
     figure out if they want to work for your company.

2. ASK ONLY JOB-RELATED QUESTIONS!
   This helps you to ask only legal questions.
   Questions such as those dealing with age,
   marital status, height, weight, or disability
   may be examples of illegal questions.

3. Ask open-ended questions (those that cannot
   be answered only with a "yes" or a "no").
   This will not only give you a chance to
   obtain more information, but will also show
   you if the candidate can "think on his(her) feet."
   Do not be afraid to follow up with another
   question to clarify an answer, or to gain more
   information.

4. Do not ask leading questions or give more
   information than is necessary at this point.
   Discussion about the position or type of
   person for which you are looking, or asking
   questions such as "You are always on time,
   aren't you?" tip off the candidate as to what you
   are looking for.

5. Ask behavioral questions about previous work
   experience rather than hypothetical questions.
   Hypothetical questions tend to encourage the
   answer that the candidate thinks you want,

rather than the real answer. For example, rather than asking, "If you were operating a machine, and it started to make funny noises, what would you do?" ask "Tell me about a time when you were operating a machine and it started to make funny noises. What did you do in that situation?"

6. NOW, give the applicant a good idea of what the job position is, and a little bit about what the company does. Give the person a chance to ask questions. Remember, this process is a two-way street. The applicant also needs information to decide whether or not (s)he wants to work for the company.

7. Tell the applicant what the next step in the hiring process is; for example, "We will be calling you within the next several days to tell you whether or not you will be hired for the position."

8. Thank the applicant for his(her) time, and see him(her) to the door.

9. Collect your thoughts, and make any notes of your impressions and observations, or other questions you may want answered before making the hiring decision.

C. What to look for during an interview

1. ability to do the job

2. ability to get along with co-workers

3. ability to adjust to the job environment

4. interest in doing the job

5. likelihood of remaining with the Company

6. potential for further growth

7. ability to keep outside factors from interfering with job performance

QUESTION	WHY ASK THAT QUESTION?
Tell me about yourself - what you've been doing and what you want to do now.	This question "breaks the ice", and lets the applicant talk about something they feel comfortable talking about. If they ask, it should be job-related.
What is your strongest point?	In addition to valuable information, this indicates level of self-confidence. A self-confident worker is a better employee.
What is your weakest point?	This usually takes more thought, but gives you more information about the level of self-confidence.
Tell me about the jobs you have had.	This gives you information you need to help you decide if the person has the necessary qualifications to do the job.
Why did you leave each job?	These answers may give clues as to person's ability, job performance, ability to get along with others, desire to do a particular job, and/or such information that the person was laid off due to the fact the company was "right-sizing" or went out of business.

QUESTION	WHY ASK THAT QUESTION?
What kind of supervisor do you work best with?	The answer here gives basic information; if the applicant doesn't work well with the kind of supervisor you are, this may not be the person you are looking for.
Rate your sense of humor on a scale of one to ten. Why do you rate yourself that way?	A good sense of humor helps in the workplace. Also, the applicant may display creativity in the answer.
Rate your honesty on a scale of one to ten. Why do you rate yourself that way?	Be suspicious if someone rates themselves as a "perfect" 10 on this one. No one is truthfully that honest. Also, watch for changes in body language or attitude that may give you a clue that something is amiss.
Rate your sense of perfection on a scale of one to ten. (How much of a perfectionist are you?) Why do you rate yourself that way?	This rating may give you some insight into the quality of work the person produces.

QUESTION	WHY ASK THAT QUESTION?
Describe your ideal job. Why?	This gives you insight into the person's creativity and ability to think on his(her) feet. Look for good reasons for the answer. The idea here is why something is said, not particularly what is said.
Why do you want to work here?	Listen for clues, such as "I know someone who works here." Follow-up questions may be a good source for references.
Why should we hire you over any other candidate with similar experience?	Again, listen for clues. An answer here may tell you about work ethic, honesty, or other skills. It also gives an indication of the level of self-confidence.

Conducting an interview can be an enjoyable and beneficial experience. Remember to do it with humor, do it legally, and do it smart. Good luck!

Good Communication: Tuning Up Your Tongue

Good communication is part of the ongoing common sense cure for stupid people syndrome in your business.

How often have you heard:

"It's all in how you say it."

It's true. How you say something can make a major difference to the person with whom you are communicating.

Verbal communication accounts for only about 7% of the meaning others will get from your speech, 38% of the meaning comes from your "vocalics" (things like intonation, inflection, and pitch), but even more important than that is the 55% accounted for by body language.

Attitude can make or break you in life, and is often reflected by all the ways you say something (verbal, vocalics, and body language).

We all know that a smile on your face in general discussion shows a positive attitude. But have you thought of how you ask (or answer) the question "Is the glass half empty, or is the glass half full?" This also can be an indication of whether you have a negative or positive attitude toward life.

Try the following exercise, listening to the inflection of your voice. It really does make a difference!

- It's *all* in how you say it.

- It's all in *how* you say it.

- It's all in how *you* say it.

- It's all in how you *say* it.

For good or ill, your conversation is your advertisement. Everytime you open your mouth you let men look into your mind. Do they see it well clothed, neat, businesswise?
Bruce Burton
(from the Poor Man's College of Quotes)

Quiz

Take the following short quiz. Think about your answers. Their implications may surprise you.

Do you say:

> I speak *at* someone.
>
> I speak *to* someone.
>
> I speak *with* someone.

Do you say:

> I'd like you to meet Mary, my wife.
>
> I'd like you to meet my wife, Mary.

Do you say:

> You didn't complete the project on time.
>
> The project is not complete.

Do you say:

> I want you to...

> Could you please...

Think about the following:

How many times have you experienced this?

You have ordered a steak in a restaurant. The server brings it to your table, and immediately says to you, "Please cut into the middle of your steak, so that I know that it is done to your liking."

What would your reaction be?

Nine-tenths of the serious controversies which result

in life result from misunderstanding.

Louis D. Brandeis

Tips and Tidbits

If a server in a restaurant asks if everything is okay, is that in fact inferring that perhaps it isn't?

If the server asks if everything is done to your liking, is that in fact what (s)he is most likely asking?

Humor is one of the best forms of communication.

Criticisms of others should, whenever possible, be made privately, and in no case should one be criticized in the presence of executives or employees of equal or lower rank.

Smile when you answer your phone. You can never tell who may be on the other end.

Say what you mean quickly and to the point. Volume of communication does not mean quality.

Speak to express, not impress.

> *It is so plain to me that eloquence, like swimming,*
> *is an art which all men might learn, though so few do.*
> *Ralph Waldo Emerson*

A helpful "tune up your tongue" method of staying on task when problem solving, doing proposals or making decisions is to use the SPIN method. This enables you to remain focused, not alienating people by becoming accusatory, cutting off their discussion, or in general, saying the wrong thing at the wrong time.

Describe the:

- **S**ituation (one sentence): The situation is (the observable behavior)...

- **P**roblem (one sentence): The problem is...

- **I**mplication: The results of this are...

- **N**eed and Payoff: We need to (suggestion for resolution)... If we do this, then...

*Half of the world is composed of people who have
something to say and can't, and the other half
who have nothing to say and keep on saying it.*

Robert Frost

The only time you should use "You" statements are when delivering compliments. For example, say "You are great!" In a not so favorable situation, instead of saying "You are late," try "I was to meet you at noon and I was concerned about you when we didn't connect."

To deal with difficult people, instead of saying "You did...you should...you need to...," try "I'm a little confused. I need help. I need clarification." Typically, given a non-judgmental opening rather than an accusation or blame, the person will generally try to help.

Use words that listeners feel as well as hear.

*The most valuable of all talents is that of never
using two words when one will do.*

Thomas Jefferson

From *The One Minute Manager* (by Blanchard and Johnson):

- Catch someone doing something right and tell them about it! (see list of *100 Ways to Say "Very Good"*)

- Use the one-minute reprimand:

    o 30 seconds of discussing the problem specifically.

    o 5 seconds of silence.

    o 25 seconds of positive reinforcement and encouragement.

On motivation through communication:

- maintain self-esteem

- listen and respond with empathy

- ask for help in solving problems

- offer help without taking responsibility

Paint pictures for your listener. For example, a canary yellow Camaro will be remembered more than a car. Someone once said that the best orator is someone who can make people see with their ears.

When speaking, maintain a personal space that is comfortable for others.

Maintain your credibility.

Speak with conviction.

Involve your listeners.

Make direct eye contact when speaking.

Every improvement in communication makes the bore
more terrible.
Frank Moore Colby

Remember!

To be most effective in the way you communicate with others:

- be open
- be honest
- be discreet
- be considerate of the other person's feelings
- be positive, even in a negative situation
- be fair
- be consistent
- **be aware of the implications of what you say, imply or do**

> *An executive can't ignore his communication*
> *any more than a driver can forget to oil his engine.*
> *Chester Burger*

You Think I Got a Bad Attitude, Buddy?

Conflict Management

What is conflict?

A conflict can be a disagreement, dispute, fight, struggle or battle having at least two sides, with those on each side thinking they are right. People perceive situations differently, and what seems like a conflict to one person may not at all be a conflict to another.

Conflict is a part of everyday life and exists in every area of our lives. At work, we may have a conflict with a peer, with a manager or subordinate, or even with a customer. How you handle the situation says a lot about you and can help determine how successful you are in life.

Conflicts are influenced by such things as:

- values and/or ethics that you developed growing up
- biases you may have developed based on
    - actual observed behaviors (reality)
    - stereotypes (perceptions)
    - decisions you have made in the past
    - something you feel extremely strongly about (emotionally charged issues or frustrations)

Is total lack of conflict good? No! In business, for instance, if there is a perception that all conflicts, or differing opinions, are bad, people may become "yes-men" and go along with something they don't necessarily agree with in order to preserve their jobs. This reduces opportunities for new ideas and for improvement of existing products, services, and methods of doing things. It may actually be harmful to the company.

Gregory E. Huszczo, Ph.D., in his book *Tools for Team Excellence*, says, "Too often there's an overemphasis on getting people to be happy and able to get along with others. Conflict shows that people care enough to speak their minds. The opposite of conflict is apathy, not peace and harmony."

Conflict can be good or bad, handled in positive or negative ways, and produce creative or destructive results.

Manage good conflict and resolve bad conflict.

Managing Good Conflict

Mark Twain once said, "It were not best that we should all think alike: it is difference of opinion that makes horse races."

In business, as we work more and more in teams, it is important to note that both good and bad conflict may occur, and probably will.

Manage good conflict in your workplace to build a better team by recognizing and using differences in people to your advantage:

- know and understand your own values, ethics, and preferences
- know and understand the values, ethics, and preferences of your teammates
- know and understand the effect you have on your teammates and that they have on you

In order to use good conflict to produce new ideas, improve old ones, and to promote a healthy work environment:

- get your teammates together
- brainstorm like crazy
- LISTEN
- reinforce new, untried ideas

Resolving Bad Conflict

Solve conflicts, not as enemies, but as friends or teammates.

Realize that there is more than one way to resolve a conflict:

- some people resolve the conflict by avoiding, or running away from it
- some people just give in and "go with the flow" – however, this approach often causes a build-up of resentment
- some people force the resolution down another's throat
- some people compromise to get a resolution
- some people collaborate in finding the best possible way to resolve a conflict. This is *usually* the best way to resolve conflict.

Steps to Resolving Conflict by Collaboration:

- be aware that a conflict may exist. (You must always be sensitive to the fact that you may be coming upon a conflict without realizing it. Be open to cues that you may receive that a conflict is coming.)

- realize the difference between interpersonal conflict (just not liking or getting along with another) and issue conflict (disagreeing about something) and try to focus on issue conflicts - the others probably won't ever be resolved.

- make a conscious decision about whether or not to confront the other person

- remember that not everything is worth fighting about - pick your battles

- confront the other person about the issue - hopefully with good communication

- choose an appropriate time and place

- determine the cause of the conflict

- get beyond immediate tensions and disagreements to the real cause of the conflict

- find out what the other person wants

- use this quick way to resolve conflict with another individual. Ask "What do you want me to do?" When asked this question, many people will respond with a less extreme demand than their original position.

- resolve the conflict
- use objective criteria
- apologize if appropriate: "I'm sorry" doesn't mean "I'm wrong"
- determine alternatives that are mutually beneficial
- use a little bit of humor
- compromise if you have to - remember, this is not an "I win - you lose" situation
- agree on a course of action that will resolve the issue or conflict most beneficially for all.
- follow-up to determine if the resolution is working

Tips for Resolving Conflict by Collaboration:

- use "cognitive restructuring" - a method of mentally converting negative aspects into positive ones by looking for the positive in a situation
- remember, if you are unsuccessful in resolving a conflict, get help from a mediator - someone you both trust and respect who will render a fair and consistent decision

Tips to Criticize Constructively:

- get the facts straight before saying anything
- choose the best timing and place - not in front of a group, and preferably in neutral territory
- don't expect to eliminate defensiveness entirely
- be fair and consistent
- avoid attacking the person - discuss the behavior objectively
- ask questions
- agree on an improved course of action
- follow-up to determine if the resolution is working

Tips for Positive Criticism:

- remember the terms respect and dignity. You want to avoid destroying a person's self-esteem while correcting a behavior.
- remember and use the "One Minute Manager" philosophies. Positive reinforcement works wonders.

How to Handle Tough Conversations:

- agree on some point - this is always the easiest way to start to handle a tough conversation. It shows the other person that you are not totally unreasonable.
- reduce finger pointing, which causes defensiveness, by reducing the use of the term "you." Talk about the issue rather than the person.
- let the person know how you feel by using the term "I."
- use the term "and" rather than "but." "But" negates the previous thought and often adds to defensiveness.

How to Handle People Who Interrupt:

- choose appropriate times and places in which you allow yourself to be interrupted. If you are interrupted at an inappropriate time, ask the other person when you can meet to talk without interruption.
- when you have something to discuss, meet in your teammate's space or territory. Then you can leave more easily when you feel the conversation is over.
- get to the point quickly
- when interrupted while speaking, try saying, "I'd like to respond to that, but first, I want to finish the point I was making."

How to Deal With People Who Know-It-All:

- don't attempt to be a know-it-all also
- ask questions rather than disagree. Know-it-alls usually love to answer questions. Often, as they answer the questions, they consider comments you have made and sometimes add them to their answers. (Just be prepared that they may also claim credit for those ideas.)

How to Cope With People Who Are Difficult to Deal With:

- kill with kindness. Be direct - but likable and polite.
- listen and respond. Allow the difficult person to fully express his or her feelings. Then acknowledge your awareness of the situation, describe what you see and hear, reveal what you think and feel, and say what you want. Tip: Don't judge or generalize (e.g. "You always do that").
- don't take a position - deal with a need. Find out what motivates a person, so you can offer alternative ways of solving the problem. Chances are the difficult person confronting you has simply adopted the most obvious solution. In other words, move from what the person wants to why the person wants it.
- accept blame. More often than not, you have played some role in bringing about the behaviors others subject you to. Admit what your fault is quickly and emphatically. Whenever you

shoulder your share of the blame, others are more likely to own up to theirs. Tip: Sometimes you can encourage the other person to cooperate by claiming more responsibility than you deserve.

Source: *What to Say to Get What You Want,* by Sam Deep and Lyle Sussman

How to Disagree Without Being Disagreeable:

- be positive and maintain that position
- be pleasant. This means smile.
- control your emotions - if they are getting out of hand, or going to get out of hand, you may want to postpone the conversation – think: appropriate timing
- decide why the other person feels the way he/she does. (see Resolving Bad Conflict) Is this interpersonal or an issue?
- listen, listen, listen
- be brief in your comments
- listen, listen, listen - (Yes, this appears above. Is that a clue to its importance?)
- use positive collaboration rather than forcing something down the other person's throat

The Role of a Mediator

Sometimes, it is necessary for a third party to act as a mediator to resolve the conflict. This person should be one whom both sides trust and respect, a person who will be fair and consistent with his/her decision. If the situation is serious enough, it might be valuable to have a trained mediator intervene. The following, however, are simple guidelines to use if you find yourself put in the role of mediator.

How to Mediate a Conflict:

- keep conflict from erupting in the first place by
  - being aware of situations, rules or guidelines
  - being aware of interpersonal conflicts (issue conflicts frequently occur more often between those who have interpersonal conflicts)
- speak separately to both parties when conflicts do occur - listen, listen, listen!!!
- speak to both parties together - listen, listen, listen!!!
- remain neutral
- get all the facts
- facilitate and explore all alternatives
- facilitate the "right" resolution
- thank both parties
- follow up to determine if the resolution is working

"One secret of success *(author's note - and this works in the process of resolving conflict)*: avoid being against anything. Instead, be for something. Instead of being against illiteracy, be for literacy. Instead of being against your company policy, be for an improved policy.

What happens: whatever you are against works against you. You begin fighting it and become a part of the problem.. But when you state what you are for, you begin focusing on the potential for positive change."

Source: *You'll See It When You Believe It*, by Dr. Wayne W. Dyer

Basic Common Sense Management Guidelines

Common sense is the cure for stupid people syndrome in your business. The SuperHero Manager stamps out stupid people syndrome whenever (s)he can.

Start using these guidelines to help cure the disease. They are very general in nature and can help your business overall. Later, we will get to some specific common sense cures to use during the daily grind.

The manager of the future, starting today, is a leader, a coach, and a counselor. (S)he also has very strong beliefs. The following are among them.

Every business success and failure is based on the actions and abilities of its people. Therefore, **hire right and manage right.**

Everyone works together.

Individuals make decisions on their own.

The system must be autocratic when necessary.

Use "Common Sense Management."

Use "Zero-based Decisions." (These are decisions based on "pure" information – no distracting circumstances – often the best decisions even when the circumstances are factored in.)

If you trusted a person enough to hire him (her), trust him (her) enough to do the job.

If it makes sense, do it.

Be positive!!! Catch an employee doing something right!!! (read Blanchard and Johnson's *One Minute Manager*)

Motivate through communication:

- maintain self-esteem

- listen and respond with empathy

- ask for help in solving problems

- offer help without taking responsibility

Believe that every employee can excel...every employee can build on his or her strengths...every employee can be a winner.

Each employee's learning experience should be active, not passive.

Strengthen a company with multicultural perspectives and gender equity.

Don't hire the first warm body, hire the right one.

Define and communicate your expectations.

Don't be too bossy. Delegate effectively.

Don't play favorites.

Be confident. Make decisions. Be consistent.

Ask for help from your employees.

Don't feel guilty about asking employees to do low-level work.

Don't suffer from the "Sinatra Syndrome." Your way is not always the most effective way.

Communicate, communicate, communicate!!!

Lead by example.

What Do You Mean I Have to Manage Them Differently?

The Boomers, the Xers and the Whys

The most commonsensical and successful method of managing is to "manage to the person." Simply put, each person is an individual and their performance can be affected positively by "managing to the person," not "managing to the group."

First, who are the boomers, the Xers and the whys? These are the three predominant groups of employees in the work force at the present time – and what better way to learn to manage an individual than to find out something about them – their values, concerns, and backgrounds? Generational management is the beginning phase of "managing to the person."

The baby boomers:

- also known as "That Generation"
- born between 1945 and 1964.
- profile:
    - grew up as children of those in the Great Depression and World War II
    - inherited the work ethic of their parents
- traits:
    - working "longer" is better
    - still follow "the rules"
    - focused on career
- stereotypes:
    - expensive: probably because they have been around for a long time!
    - think they know it all - you probably would, too, if you have been around for a long time!

- don't understand and don't care to understand technology: we got along fine without it up to now – why start?
- don't want to change their ways – see above

- how to manage:
  - respect

The Xers:

- also known as the X Generation and the Millenial
- born between 1964 and 1976 or 1965 and 1981
- profile:
  - raised with technology
  - "latch-key" kids – parents both working – had to fend for themselves
  - want to achieve quality of life that in many cases had eluded their parents
  - relationships are important
- traits: due to their perception of growing up seeing their boomer parents taken advantage of by employers
  - not comfortable with rules and/or authority
  - independent and entrepreneurial
  - flexibility is "king"
  - technologically skilled

- o value honesty
- o want to give input
- o value diversity
- o possess weakening work ethic
- o have different conversational styles
  - ▪ X-ers grew up on sound bites, so at times they can be very abrupt. They also may perceive older people, that's us, folks, as taking forever to make a point, and may appear to be bored with what we're saying. "Make the point, and get on with it!"
  - ▪ X-ers are comfortable with silence. Understand those silences. Boomers grew up in crowded families and classrooms and expect noise and conversation. X-ers, on the other hand, often grew up in smaller families and had to occupy themselves in front of the TV or computer. Silence, to them, is okay.
- stereotypes:
  - o lazy
  - o attention span of a "gnat" - very short attention span

o   want their own way

o   whiners and slackers

o   "You owe me."

o   "I need weekends off."

o   "I'm late today because I partied too late last night."

o   "I deserve a pay raise because I've been here for two weeks."

o   arrogant – must build *themselves* up because they have no real role models of success. Previous generations had their parents as role models – and role models could be found in many other places, even including the comic books that were read for fun. Characters such as Superman and Superboy may have had superpowers, but they also demonstrated strong values and work ethics. They were the epitome of success.

- how to manage:

    o   train in new skills – train, train, train!

    o   constant feedback

    o   make work meaningful

    o   include in decision making

    o   be flexible in scheduling time off, work hours, and working from home

    o   include as part of the team, particularly in decision-making

The Whys:

- also known as the Y Generation and the Echo Boomers
- born between 1977 and 1994 or 1982 and 2000
- profile:
    - like to volunteer
    - want time to be their own
    - social media incredibly important
    - many y's maintain technical social contact all day at work
    - desire constant feedback
    - raised by parents who in many cases gave constant praise or rewarded for behaviors that should have been expected
    - very ethnically diverse now – will continue to become more diverse in coming years
- traits:
    - very computer savvy
    - not as socially oriented as the other groups
        - like to work independently because they often were raised in one-parent families, or two parent families with both parents working, with much time spent in day care – prefer to communicate through social media, as opposed to "face to face"
    - eager to learn

o looking to make themselves a valuable commodity

o changing jobs is not an issue

o believe in work/lifestyle balance

o often find a place they would like to live, then find a job, as opposed to boomers and X-ers who find a job, then a place to live

o will sometimes take a job to be with friends

o will challenge authority

o loyalty to themselves - what's in it for me?

o recognition and positive reinforcement are important

o often still "managed" by their parents (helicopter parents)

o because they grew up in "Internet Age," instant gratification is a significant trait, constant stimulation important

o good multi-taskers

- how to manage:

  o train using computer and on-line

  o telecommuting important

OKAY, now you know the differences in generational traits, how will you be successful in managing different people in different generations?

Managing across multiple generations effectively begins with understanding each employee's values, expectations and goals. To do that, you must:

- set aside your own system of values and expectations and not try to impose yours on them. We must first change *our* mindsets. We cannot manage like we have in the past and expect to succeed. We must be willing to manage well and manage the individual, not the group. We must be open to change. The days of "My way or the highway" are over with!
- be aware that the stereotypes present today of different generations are often not true. You must have the courage to look beyond those stereotypes to understand the different values, expectations and goals.

Then, you must remember, always "manage to the individual" rather than "manage to the group."

Two concepts must be mastered in order to be successful with any workforce:

1. hire right
2. manage right

Easy, right? Each of these concepts is based on common sense and the two basic watchwords of human resources: always be *fair* and *consistent!*

Hire right!

- realize that forty percent of hiring decisions are made on the basis of appearance factors alone. Obviously, this can be a problem!
- look for two things in hiring:
    - ability or capability to do job
    - attitude (culture match) - skills can be trained, so hire for attitude
- ask open-ended questions in the employment interview that tell something about the person
- "off-the- wall" questions work nicely also to tell something about the person
- ask many behavioral questions, rather than all hypothetical
    - rather than ask, "What would you say to a customer that...," you may want to ask, "Describe to me a situation in which a customer...Tell me what you did and what you said in this instance."
- describe the job and company after you are done asking questions so you don't tip off the applicant as to what you're looking for
- listen carefully to answers
- check references

Manage right!

- On managing in general:
  - be fair
  - be consistent
  - use common sense
- On managing your employees:
  - go to your employee's strengths
  - set expectations early and often
  - empower your employees
  - trust your employees
- delegate, delegate, delegate
- make your employees accountable
- give feedback
- listen to your employees. They know the answers.
- reinforce work ethic
  - research on work ethic over the past fifteen years identifies the "soft skills" (or employability skills) that we tend to think of as work ethic as:
    - dependability/responsibility
    - positive attitude toward work
      - conscientiousness, punctuality, efficiency
      - interpersonal skills, cooperation, working as a team member
      - self-confidence, positive self-image

- adaptability, flexibility

- enthusiasm, motivation

- self-discipline, self—management

- appropriate dress, grooming

- honesty, integrity

- ability to work without supervision

- model appropriate work ethic

- remember, what you perceive as lack of work ethic may only be and probably is, an indication of a different work ethic. Respect their style, even if it's not yours.

- reward employees for exceptional work

- reward them often, but appropriately (don't reward for the sake of rewarding) being specific about the behavior being rewarded

- promote qualified employees

- train them for their next job

- assign them a variety of tasks

- value their work

- On managing thinking:

  - demand critical thinking and encourage creative thinking
  - ask the question: "What are we really trying to do...(solve, discover, change, fix)?"
  - think "outside the box"
  - use the principles of CPI (Continuous Process Improvement).
  - be flexible
  - if it makes sense, do it

- On managing through communication:

  - maintain self-esteem
  - listen and respond with empathy
  - ask for help in solving problems
  - offer help without taking responsibility
  - explain the why behind what you're requesting employees to do. For example, tell them why it is important for them not to chew gum while taking a customer's order. Explain the benefits both for the company and for them.
  - talk with your employees. Let them know you're willing to listen to their ideas. Most importantly, talk with them

like they are human beings. Communicate, communicate, communicate!

- On managing *YOU*:

  - practice your people skills
    - set an example for your employees. You can't expect an employee to do something you don't. Expect them to do as you do, not as you say.
    - make your employees your customers. Serve them and give them all the help you can.
  - manage to the individual, not the group
  - lighten up! Have a sense of humor.
  - do the right thing
  - create a workplace where people want to be, and they will come and do their best. Start thinking of your workforce as volunteers who elect to come to work or not. Create an atmosphere of enthusiasm for success.
  - use simplified training programs that ensure the success of the employee. Use videos, webinars, online training, simplified manuals and lists whenever appropriate.
  - be flexible. Notice that this appears above also.
  - if it looks like they're not going to succeed, look in the mirror and ask yourself if you have spent as much time as possible with them, and if you have done everything possible to make them a success.

The Common Sense
Decision Making Flow Chart

Making everyday decisions for your business can be very difficult – you want to make the most effective decision that will produce the best result for your organization. Basing your decisions on common sense can enhance every decision you make and help make you a SuperHero Manager.

Use the following flow chart as a guideline for making a common sense based decision. It can be used in any circumstance, and after you have been following it for awhile, it will become second nature – you won't even have to think about it!

The Common Sense Decision Making Flow Chart

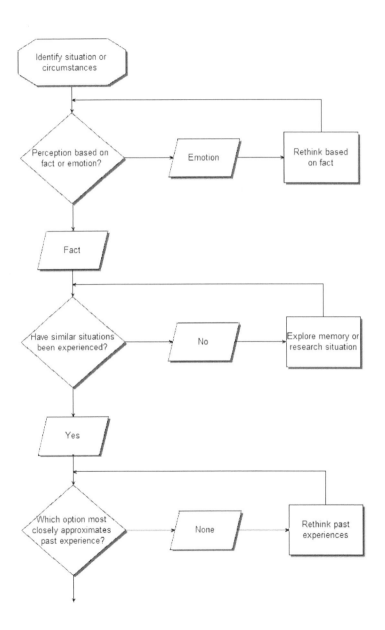

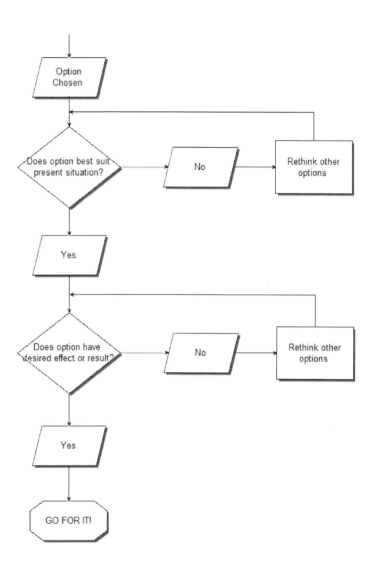

Getting Your Employees to
Use Common Sense

How do you get common sense?

To program or re-program your brain to use common sense, you must practice, practice, practice! Common sense, in particular, and your brain, in general, can be exercised like a muscle, by doing logic puzzles and puzzles involving manipulation of shapes. (Jigsaw puzzles come to mind.) Common sense is also developed through your experiences and/or your exposure to someone else's experiences.

How to figure out the "commonsensical solution" to situations and/or circumstances

Step 1: *PASTTHINK*

Think of a similar situation either you have experienced yourself, or have been exposed to. Be sure that your perception of the situation is based on fact, rather than emotion. Compare the situation with your memory of past experience. This often happens without conscious thought.

Step 2: *NOWTHINK*

Think of options to use in this situation. Assimilate the present facts, consider the alternatives, and compare with past experiences. Come to a conclusion about which option is the most viable.

Step 3: *FUTURETHINK*

Determine if the present situation will deviate from past experience during the application of the chosen option. Determine the implications of the option you have chosen. What effect will the option chosen have upon the situation? If this is the desired outcome, then GO FOR IT!

So, how do you get your employees to use common sense?

Model It:

- lead by example (role model)—including the sweat factor (work ethic)
- practice what you preach — working through problems and learning from your mistakes
- use your own common sense first
- give or show specific examples of common sense in action—bringing experience to life

Expect It:

- require communication
- make it an understood philosophy of doing business, not just an ideal/desired goal
- preach practicing, applying, and implementing as a daily function of the job

Encourage It:

- remind them to persevere in making common sense decisions and that persistence and hard work will pay off

- create an atmosphere of enthusiasm for success
- be supportive, offering guidance when necessary, but don't do it for them. They must do it to learn it themselves.
- explain the benefits both for company and individual—simplicity, clarification & improvement
    - company: efficiency, productivity, problem solving, foresight, simplification, practicality, customer service and satisfaction, morale and profit
    - individual: self-confidence, worth and esteem; deduction & reasoning ability; judgment for problem solving and decision making skills; self-reliance and independence

Acknowledge It:

- be involved, know what's going on around you
- applaud the effort, whenever possible
- praise hard work and persistence—not just outcomes
- make praise specific; don't just offer generic esteem boosting
- reprimand in private and praise in public. Everyone likes a pat on the back.
- review and discuss the situation and its outcome
    - Was the result the desired outcome?
    - What was done correctly?
    - Was there anything that could have been done differently?

Reinforce It:

- respect their style, even if it's not your style
- allow mistakes to be made, as they are opportunities to learn to do something better
- support its use, even if the best decision/choice wasn't made
- let them try it their own way first—unless their work suffers or the results are unacceptable
- create a reward system

Teach It:

- build the foundation first—don't jump ahead
- get a commitment to learning—creatively challenge curiosity
- provide thorough training specific to their job, including a comprehensive and complete orientation
- make learning a daily part of the process to improve skills and to take pleasure in the effort, not just in the achievement
- develop the ability to learn to ask probing questions—not just surface questions
- create a broad 'fund of knowledge'
- develop a mentor program
- role play to provide the power of practice
- build a support network
- think first – then act!

Remember:

Common sense is genius dressed in working clothes.

Ralph Waldo Emerson

Running a Commonsensical Business

Running a "commonsensical business" is not always easy. It IS the hallmark of a SuperHero Manager. The first rule of thumb is to simplify, simplify, simplify! Reduce everything to its lowest common denominator – then start making decisions.

In running a "commonsensical business," the "common sense flow chart" is a very simple process to follow for making general decisions.

In addition, there are two types of "commonsensical business" cures for any symptoms of stupid people syndrome in your business:

- those for general business challenges
- those that deal with people – namely, employees

First, easy cures for general business challenges:

- make "zero-based decisions" that are based on "pure" information with no distracting circumstances. These are often the best decisions even when the circumstances are factored in.
- if it makes sense, do it
- learn your product
- learn your competition
- work harder and/or smarter than anyone else
- build relationships - the more people you stay in touch with, the more people who remember you, the more relationships you build, the more sales you get
- work the prospects, not the sales

- focus on benefits as opposed to features to close a sale. People respond more to benefits (What's in it for me – WIIFM) than to features.
- ask questions to overcome objections during a sale. Is it a negative decision because:
  - money is an issue
  - the person you are talking with is not the decision maker
  - there is just no need or interest
  - "your company is just no good"

Next, easy management cures for employee challenges:

Hire Right!

- don't hire the first warm body, hire the right one
- ask the right questions
- do the reference checks
- don't lead with company info
- put together the "pieces of the jigsaw puzzle" before hiring

Manage Right!

The Manager of the Future is a leader, a coach and a counselor. (S)he also has very strong beliefs. The following are among them:

- manage to the person, not the group
- tune up your tongue
- use positive reinforcement
- know your numbers
- make sure everyone works together
- allow individuals to make decisions on their own
- be autocratic when necessary
- use "Common Sense Management"
- trust your employee to do the job, if you trusted him (her) enough to hire him (her)
- be positive!!! Catch an employee doing something right!!! (from *The One Minute Manager* by Blanchard and Johnson)
- motivate through communication
    - maintain self-esteem
    - listen and respond with empathy
    - ask for help in solving problems
    - offer help without taking responsibility